WestBow Press books may be ordered through booksellers or by contacting:

WestBow Press
A Division of Thomas Nelson
1663 Liberty Drive
Bloomington, IN 47403
www.westbowpress.com
1-(866) 928-1240

Because of the dynamic nature of the Internet, any web addresses or links contained in this book may have changed since publication and may no longer be valid. The views expressed in this work are solely those of the author and do not necessarily reflect the views of the publisher, and the publisher hereby disclaims any responsibility for them.

Any people depicted in stock imagery provided by Thinkstock are models, and such images are being used for illustrative purposes only.

Certain stock imagery © Thinkstock.

ISBN: 978-1-4497-6598-9 (sc)
ISBN: 978-1-4497-6599-6 (e)
Library of Congress Control Number: 2012916258

Printed in the United States of America

WestBow Press rev. date: 09/05/2012

The
BELIEVER'S RESOURCE
for SPIRITUAL VICTORY
and RENEWAL

REV. DAREN S. LESTER

WESTBOW
PRESS
A DIVISION OF THOMAS NELSON

Dedication

I dedicate this book to my late father, Danny Jack Lester, who was a founding pillar throughout my life.

Contents

Introduction

In the 21ˢᵗ century, there has been a renewed interest in the spiritual realm. Sadly, not all of this interest is in the form of searching for God or His Son Jesus Christ, but it is in channeling, a search of spiritism, witchcraft, New Age philosophy or some other pagan source.

This book that I have written seeks to send the believer to a direct conduit to the Lord Jesus Christ. It is my intention to empower the believer to a spiritually-based knowledge on how to overcome the attacks of the enemy and live a victorious Christian walk in the daily shadow of the Cross.

I John 1:1 "That which was from the beginning, which we have heard, which we have seen with our eyes, which we have looked upon, and our hands have handled, of the Word of life;"

Rev. Daren S. Lester

CHAPTER ONE

TRADITIONS: DEALING WITH ISSUES THAT WILL HINDER YOUR SPIRITUAL VICTORY

When I was seeking the leading of the Lord for this book, I began to ask Him, 'What do you want me to write? How do you want me to say it? What order should I arrange these chapters that I might achieve maximum impact for your Kingdom, oh Lord Jesus?'

Then, the Lord spoke and answered me in three different methods. First, I was watching a couple of well-known and highly respected ministers on television teaching on the gifts of the Holy Spirit. And while they were discussing the varying aspects about it in the believers' lives, the Lord gave me an open revelation that I had never thought of before. He allowed me to see the need to stop elevating man's traditions to the same point of authority as Scripture.

Later on that week, I went out for lunch with a local minister to speak and plan on how we might launch a new work for the Lord in our local community. Before you know it, I heard both he and I speaking about the various church traditions that we had both grew up with. Suddenly thereafter, it felt like a ball of lightning had struck my spirit yet again. God's Spirit spoke softly to me and said, "Did you hear me, Daren?"

Lastly, I went to pray that next evening and the Lord said, 'Traditions'. So, I had asked the Lord, "how should I put all of this?" And He said, "Just speak openly, honestly and directly. Do not hold anything back. My people are battling daily and many of them lose daily and get defeated almost to the point of backsliding because of traditions."

Now, to be honest, it is not my intention to smash all traditions because in fact many traditions are good and serve a purpose. But, many traditions are not God-given. They are instead dictated by men and become a battleground that many sincere believers cannot live up to because they are not inspired by the Holy Spirit. They are contrived by a hidden demonic hierarchy that seeks to discourage or destroy as many as they can ensnare by a religious dictate and not a Christ-centered doctrine.

As I was doing my studies on traditions, I found that according to the Crudens Complete Concordance that the word 'tradition' usually means 'laws and regulations handed down orally from one generation to another and forming the oral law of the Jews which Jesus regularly denounced when it was against the real law of God.' Think about that. How many times have you heard a preacher preach something he had heard or was taught, but it wasn't found in the Bible? It's like the oral tradition of the Jews. They had elevated up to the same authority as the written Word of God. How many times have you had a minister preach what was on his heart instead of what was in the Word?

When I started seeking God's face for help and direction to write this book, He gave me insight as to what the first three chapters should be. As I sought His direction, He lead me as to the order that each of the chapters should be written and what subjects to touch on first. When I had asked Him why I should start out by dealing with traditions, God said, "because traditions have lead more souls astray, kept more people bound and caused more souls to be cast into Hell than anything else in history, except for refusing Jesus Christ as one's personal Lord and Savior."

Let's take a few moments to view just a few traditions that the early church had to deal with and then we will confront some traditions that have been hindering Christian believers for the past several years:

Matthew 15:2 says, 'Why do your disciples transgress the tradition of the elders? For they wash not their hands when they eat bread.' This is a clear example of an oral Jewish tradition being elevated by men to the point of the Ten Commandments dictated and given by God.

The commandments of God i.e. laws were given from God to man for the purpose of pointing out sin and how to be removed from the penalty of sin. On the other hand, the oral Pharisaical tradition of the counsel of the Sanhedrin was elevated through a process of time due to an establishment of continuing changing rules and regulations of the Jewish religious authorities at any given time which means even if you followed the simple rule of washing your hands, they could've came up with another tradition of the elders no matter how vague or inconsequential that you may not have followed or known.

Mark 7:5 says, 'Then the Pharisees and the scribes asked him, Why walk not Your Disciples according to the tradition of the Elders, but eat bread with unwashed hands?'

Matthew 15:3, 'But He answered and said unto them, Why do you also transgress the commandment of God by your tradition?' Simply put, Jesus, tiring of answering non-ending questions about religious traditional laws simply replied, he would not validate the traditions of man but emphasized the Word of God. One leads to salvation and one leads to damnation.

Mark 7:9 says, 'And He said unto them, Full well you reject the Commandment of God, that you may keep your own tradition.' In this verse, Jesus emphasizes that men prefer their own teachings to that of God's because man's can change from day to day, but God's won't.

Now, as to speaking to the point of traditions that have kept the church our Lord and Savior Jesus Christ down and divided.

I have preached in several churches for twenty-six years from various denominational to non-denominational organizations. I was raised in a Christian home with two God-fearing parents and two younger brothers. I went for seven years to a private Christian school and then to a private Christian college. I truly know a lot about traditions from these experiences. Still not enough, you may say?

Well, when I got married, my wife's father, mother and extended family were Catholics that became gloriously saved. Jesus Christ lead them out of bondage to salvation. I started and pastored a church and had to deal with various traditions of men at various times. Here are some traditions that you may be dealing with:

Catholic Tradition - 'Once baptized in the church you are always saved.' Scriptures to refute this are John 14:6, Acts 16:30-31, Romans 5:8, Romans 6:23, Ephesians 2:8-9.

1 John 1:7 and Revelations 3:20. If you had viewed the mentioned Scriptures, you can clearly see that God is willing to receive us unto Himself if we simply follow the Heavenly mandate and repent of our sins and ask the Lord Jesus Christ into our heart and make Him the Lord and Savior of our lives. Then and only then are we in the true church.

Old-Time Pentecostal Tradition - 'Do as we do and dress as we do or you are not in the church of the Lord.' Scriptures to refute this are John 3:16, Revelations 3:20, Acts 16:31, Romans 3:23 and Ephesians 2:8-9. If you notice the blessed simplicity of the gospel message, many of these Scriptures were used to refute the last tradition.

God's Word is eternal. The name of the denomination may change, the oral tradition may change, but it is still a man-contrived law. God's law is the ultimate and supreme authority. If any of man's traditions do not stand up to the scrutiny of God's law, then it is another piece of chaff in the wind.

United Pentecostal Tradition - 'If you are not baptized and speaking in tongues, you are not saved.' Scriptures to refute this are John 14:15-19, Luke 11:13, Acts 1:4-5(Please Note: With this Scripture, these people were not only already called to salvation by the Holy Spirit, but were waiting to be filled by the power of the Holy Spirit), Acts 2:1-4, Acts 10:44-48(Please Note: Dealing with Cornelius, his household and those in attendance hearing the message that Peter was delivering that while Peter was preaching, the Holy Spirit fell upon the audience without an altar call prior to water baptism and irrespective of race, rank, gender or creed) and Acts 19:2,6.

Various Denominations Tradition - 'If you preach the Bible by itself and not our doctrinal statements, then you are not preaching at all.' Scripture to refute this is 2 Timothy 2:15-19.

<u>Baptist Tradition</u> - 'Once saved, always saved.' Scriptures to refute this are Psalms 51:9-15, Isaiah 1:18-20, Isaiah 55:7, Hosea 14:1-4, Hebrews 7:25 and 1 John 1:9.

<u>Methodist and Wesleyan Tradition</u> - 'If you speak in tongues other than known human tongues, then you are possessed of the devil.' Scriptures to refute this are Isaiah 28:11-12, Matthew 3:11, Acts 2:4, Acts 8: 14-17, Acts 10:44-46, I Corinthians 14:39 and Jude 20.

Let me say that not all of these traditions are held by every church or majority of the aforementioned groups of believers. These are traditions that I have had to face and contend with in various areas of ministry. I feel it is important to say that traditions held by a believer can make or break that believer if it is held up as gospel and without a gospel foundation. It is important that any doctrine, tradition, practice or belief be founded solely upon the gospel of our Lord Jesus Christ.

Notes

CHAPTER TWO

DEALING WITH ISSUES
OF MORALITY IN YOUR LIFE

When thinking on this chapter and asking the Lord what to exactly say, I came to the conclusion that one of the biggest hindrances for most Christians in obtaining spiritual victory are issues of morality. Moral issues will make or break your walk with God. Those same issues will oftentimes determine if you live an overcoming spiritual walk or you seem to dwell in the same areas of your life in a spiritual malaise.

Spiritual victory is a must for any Christian minister, but it is just as important for the layperson in the church. Both ministers and laypersons have lost their witness for the Lord due to some failure in their moral lives. Our private moral lives speak more to our Christian walk and faith in Christ than perhaps any other aspect of our day to day witness to the world.

What we do in secret eventually is broadcasted to those we seek to save in the name of the Lord Jesus. We in our failings give occasion for the enemies of the cross to speak ill of the redemptive, saving, renewing power of the blood of Jesus Christ. What they fail to realize is that the blood of Jesus has never lost its power but rather we the church have failed to live in the fullness of God's benefits that were provided to us by means of the fulfilled work that Jesus accomplished at the cross.

We were the ones that fell short of God's potential victory that was provided to us at the cross of Calvary. All that we had to do was to tell our flesh the word no. Take a moment and look at yourself in the mirror and ask this question. 'Did I fail because God wasn't with me or because I wanted to do what I wanted to do more than subjugate my will to the will of God?' Many times we refuse to tell ourselves no because we want to please our flesh more than we want to yield ourselves to God. This desire we portray deals with a sanctification issue.

Let us look at the most important moral issues that keep the most people from having a God-inspired, Heaven ordained, victorious Christian walk:

Alcoholism-Firstly, I will be starting out with Scriptures that encourage you to overcome the addiction that alcohol brings. Psalms 27:14, 'Wait on the Lord: be of good courage, and He shall strengthen thine heart: wait, I say, on the Lord.' This verse plainly tells us that if the believer sits still in faith, that the Lord will come by in due time and strengthen his heart that he might overcome his battles. But not only that, it tells you in a secret reference that many readers will overlook that God gives you a secret weapon of strength by you encouraging yourself.

Psalms 34:6, 'This poor man cried, and the Lord heard him, And saved him out of all his troubles.' In this verse, note the words 'poor man'. Each soul that is in a desperate battle to overcome a weakness, failure, addiction, or possessive issue is viewed from the Lord's point of view as a individual in poverty. When one cries out to the Lord, he comes as one that pays the debts incurred from our sin. And in so doing He delivers us from all of our troubles whether physical, emotional, mental or ultimately spiritual.

Psalms 46:1, 'God is our refuge and strength, A very present help in trouble.' This verse when viewed in the truest sense tells you not to be self-reliant, trust in self-help or to count on your own self-esteem to be an overcomer. It tells us that God is the Source of our strength. God is the one that provides a safe harbor in the time of storm. When trouble is currently about you, He is in the time called present with you. Another words, when the storms are raging, He is there to be the small still voice that can quiet the storm. If that is not enough, He is the boat upon which the waves rock. If that is still not enough, He will be the life preserver that goes around your chest, arms and under your head and neck. And though the waves roar, you will never be dipped below the point of being able to spiritually breathe the air of God. He will not allow you to drown, He will not allow you to be capsized or trapped underneath the wreckage of your life if you rely upon Him and His power and His fulfilled promises that were accomplished at the Cross of Calvary.

Let's now deal with a few verses that tells us what happens to the seeker of God if they do not overcome their battles with alcoholic beverages. This may not be an instantaneous defeat, but as time progresses, you will either overcome it or it will overcome you.

Proverbs 20:1, 'Wine is a mocker, strong drink is raging: And whoever is deceived thereby is not wise.'

Isaiah 5:11, 'Woe unto them that rise up early in the morning, that they may follow strong drink.'

If we view these two verses in context, you can see unless you are just totally blind the stance that Scripture takes against alcoholic beverages. The problem with these beverages is that people do things they normally would not do, they are not in control, they are encumbered and impaired and more often than not are placed in compromising positions. People that drink sometimes have a totally different personality. A nice person can become an angry person at the drop of a hat. A serious person can become a jester to all that are around. If you notice the second verse, God uses the word 'woe'. That word is a sincere warning because it gives an implied thought that a person that drinks during the night or a weekend in order to deal with the consequences of the past evening drinks to start the day. The Bible clearly states, 'Thou shalt have no other gods before me.' What you do in the start of your day usually determines the course of your day.

Isaiah 26:3 is a good verse to read along with Isaiah 41:10 and Habakkuk 2:15. Let's read Romans 14:21. 'It is good neither to eat flesh, nor to drink wine, nor anything whereby thy brother stumbleth, or is offended, or is made weak.' I basically have given you this verse as a basis for those of you out there that play that old, outdated argument that is just Old Testament. The New Testament quite obviously has several verses condemning the use of alcohol as well. It tells us in this verse that our addictions may not just damn our own souls to Hell, but we may be a stumbling block or hindrance to a brother or sister that looks to us as an example or a source of spiritual strength. Have you ever thought that you may be the only light that someone else may see in the time of their storm? If that is the case, will you be a life raft that God can use you as an instrument to rescue a person in the time of storm or will you be the reefs that are hidden under the water that may cause that person to spiritually sink that is around you?

Here are some verses for you as the reader that may not agree with the aforementioned statements. Ephesians 5:18 and Philippians 3:13-14. Now, I know that in many modern day churches you may be told that drinking is not a sin, but if it is not a sin, then why do so many people deal with the addiction of it? The answer to this is because it is a venue by which Satan uses to ensnare victims and keep them in bondage. If the Bible says don't, then don't. If your church says that this is just a stupid old-time belief, then who will you follow? A man or God's Word? If you want freedom and victory, then follow God's Word and find another Bible-believing church because yours is backslidden if they do not accept God's Word as-is.

As of late, I talked to a man that told me he believes that even if a person is backslidden if they die, they will still go to Heaven, but they will not receive any spiritual gifts, rewards, or crowns.

Dear reader, let me tell you here and now that this is a teaching from Hell. If you are backslidden, you will and are going to Hell to be eternally separated from God. You indeed will not receive any gifts, but for that matter, you will not even get in the front gate of Heaven because you are either saved or you are not. Matthew chapter 25 is a good example for you to read. You are either a sheep or a goat. God doesn't have any other classes in Heaven.

Scriptures that deal with a backslidden state for you to read are Psalms 51:10-12 and Philippians 3:13-14. Let us read now Isaiah 1:18, 'Come now, and let us reason together, saith the Lord: Though your sins be as scarlet, they shall be as white as snow; though they be red like crimson, they shall be as wool.' Isaiah 55:7, 'Let the wicked forsake his way, and the unrighteous man his thoughts; and let him return to the Lord, And he will have compassion on him, and to our God, for He will abundantly pardon.' Hosea 14:4, 'I will heal their backsliding, I will love them freely, For mine anger is turned away from him.'

Hebrews 7:25, 'Wherefore He is able also to save them to the uttermost that come unto God by Him, seeing He ever liveth to make intercession for them.' I John 1:9, 'If we confess our sins, He is faithful and just to forgive us our sins, and to cleanse us from all unrighteousness.'

Just viewing these verses should tell you that there are only two categories of people in God's viewpoint. There are saved and unsaved. If you are saved, you strive to leave sin behind and the sin nature. If you are unsaved, then the sin nature rules and reigns without any resistance. A backslider in essence is a redeemed person that has turned their back upon the laws of God. The laws of God that drew him by the Holy Spirit to the understanding of the finished work of the Cross that Jesus Christ completed by His death, burial and resurrection and now for whatever reason chooses to denounce by his or her lifestyle.

If you read in Revelations 3:15, 'I know thy works, that thou art neither cold nor hot: I would that thou wert cold or hot.' Verse 16 continues as saying, 'So then because thou art lukewarm: and neither cold nor hot, I will spue thee out of my mouth.' I would like for you to take a moment to view these last two verses especially. For anyone to say a backslidden person can go to Heaven but he or she will not receive gifts is on the verge of being a reprobate according to the Scriptures. If you read the entirety of chapter 3 of Revelations and combine it with the entirety of Matthew chapter 25, you can clearly see people saying, 'Lord, I knew you.' But God replies, 'I never knew thee' because they left their personal relationship with Him back at the Cross. God doesn't recognize your past seniority with Him. He only views your current condition through the prism of the Blood of Christ and your relationship to Him concurrent upon your faithfulness to be obedient to the works He has set out before you.

Let's look at the word 'lust'. We all know this word but the Bible most often infers this word to mean as 'seeking pleasure or desire with no idea of evil.' The way I read it is 'seeking pleasure with desire with no thought or regard to evil.' But, as you know, today lust is a huge issue everywhere with all of the movies, TV shows, CD's, magazines and media that bombard our daily lives. That should drive us to seek a closer walk with God and enter into a personal renewing of our spirits daily. But what is this lust that the Bible speaks of? How does it stick its claws into us? James 1:14 gives us a hint. 'But every man is tempted, when he is drawn away of his own lust and enticed.' The NIV version of the Bible reads it as this: 'But each one is tempted, by his own evil desire, he is dragged away and enticed.' Verse 15 continues with this thought and reads as follows, 'Then, after desire has conceived, it gives birth to sin: and sin, when it is full grown, gives birth to death.'

The Bible verses that we just read tells us what causes us to be ensnared in lust. It is our own personal drawings. What you lust after may not affect me. What draws me may bounce right off of you. When one looks at the word lust, it can really be broken down into the thought of individual desire. If you have a tendency for a wrongful desire, then it is incumbent upon you to avoid situations in which you might put that desire in a place to tempt you to yield to it. Here are a few verses that you may desire to read that can fill you in more fully on how to deal with and what to look for concerning lust:

Romans 1:27, Galatians 5:16, I John 2:16, Matthew 5:28, I Corinthians 10:6, Galatians 5:17, Romans 1:24, 2

Timothy 2:22 and 2 Timothy 4:3. As you can see in these aforementioned verses, there are all kinds of lust that may draw us away from God's intended plan. The lust of the flesh, lust of spirit, lust of power and various other desires which ultimately lead to our destruction if not dealt with in accordance to God's plan. But, remember, God always makes a way of escape from every temptation and will give us the ultimate victory if we look to Him as our Source in dealing with our daily issues. A good verse that supports this is Hebrews 10:23.

Notes

 ## CHAPTER THREE

ISSUES OF FAITHLESSNESS AND THE NEGATIVE ASPECTS IT WILL HAVE ON YOUR SPIRITUAL WALK

One of the major factors that you will face and thus ultimately determine whether you keep and maintain spiritual victory in your life or not is how you approach issues of faith. A good definition of faith is, "Faith is a dependence on the veracity of another." "Firm belief or trust in a person, thing or doctrine."

These are just a few definitions of faith in a broad sense and are found in Crudens Concordance. But, of course, there are other types of faith as well but they all boil down to our trust and faith in God, His Word, His character and His being.

If we have faith, nothing can overcome us but if we lack faith, then we cannot overcome anything. Let's look and see what happens when we have a faith issue in our lives. When we have an issue with faith, we do not believe in essence what God says. We are in truth denying God's Word, our belief in Him, His act He fulfilled upon the Cross as well as His promises to us. We are denying His ability to empower us with the Holy Spirit.

So, when you are faithless, you are telling God that you do not depend upon Him. Nor do you believe, trust or rely upon Him, His Word or the empowering of the Holy Spirit. You do not believe that He is able to keep or fulfill any of His verbal or written promises that He has made to you or the church.

Why do I write this? It's simple. If we do not believe God now, then how can we rely upon Him in the future? God is eternal and His promises are everlasting for those of us that choose to believe in Him.

I could fill this book with Scriptures pointing to the faithfulness of God, but I am asking you to do a personal study on what the Bible says as to the faithfulness of God and then keep studying and begin to apply it to your daily walk with our Lord and Savior.

Let me give you a few Scriptures that deal with people that were faithless in the Bible and let us see how Jesus viewed them.

Mark 9:19 says, 'He answered him, and said, O faithless generation, how long shall I be with you? How long shall I suffer you? Bring him unto me.' The problem represented by a lack of faith by those around Jesus at this time in any other person standing at that position dealing with those circumstances would have caused a lack of spiritual power that could have been used to deliver the son of the man that was possessed by devils. The lack of faith was so evident in the entirety of the community where the man lived, that Jesus referred to the entire city as a group that had a generational faith problem. This problem was so evident that Jesus asked those around Him two questions. The first question is, 'How long shall I be with you?' Jesus being the Son of God knew of His limited time to work physically upon the earth.

He was asking them in essence, 'how long do I have to instill confidence in you to accept God's Word at face value?' The second question was, 'how long shall I suffer you?' This could be understood to read, 'how long until you simply understand who I am and what I can do?'

John 20:27 says, 'Then said he to Thomas, Reach hither your finger, and behold My Hands; and reach hither your hand, and thrust it into my side: and be not faithless, but believing.' Now, as you can see, Jesus had just appeared to the disciples. Those that had seen Him, walked with Him and beheld his miracles struggled to maintain their faith. Notice that Jesus when confronting Thomas about his own personal faithlessness used Thomas's own words to confront him personally that He might challenge his faith. When Jesus had told Thomas to touch His hands and feel His side, the word He ended with was 'believe'. This means simply 'have faith'. After this demonstration of power by the Lord Jesus Christ, we never hear of Thomas ever doubting Him again.

Let's view a few more verses that may tell you why you struggle to maintain your personal faith.

Luke 17:5 says, 'And the Apostles said unto the Lord, Increase our faith.' If you notice the apostles requested that the Lord 'increase their faith'. If you struggle with faith and have continuous faith issues, then a good place to start is to ask the Lord to help you to be placed in positions where your faith will grow and flourish. Oftentimes this means trials, testings and sometimes tribulations because God has to move you beyond your own abilities, power, reason and resources into an area where He is your Source and totality. But if we read verse 6, 'And the Lord said, If you had faith as a grain of mustard seed, you might say unto this sycamine tree, Be thou plucked up by the root, and be thou planted in the sea; and it should obey you.' Jesus answered their requests with a simple statement. If you have but the smallest amount of faith, you can move and impact the world around you.

Romans 4:12 says, 'And the Father of Circumcision to them that are not of Circumcision only but who also walk in the steps of that Faith of our father Abraham which he had being yet uncircumcised.' Though many that were of Jewish background had faith in the act of circumcision, this verse tells us that Abraham had faith beyond the act of circumcision. He was an example to us of one that had faith unto salvation and that his faith was imputed to him by God as righteousness. Genesis 15:6 is the verse that tells us of this.

Here are a few verses for you to read to study about faith and how to deal with faithlessness in your life as others did in their walk with God whether challenged by the apostles, prophets or God Himself.

Romans 10:8, Romans 10:17(tells us how we obtain faith on a continuing basis), Romans 12:3, I Corinthians 13:2,

Ephesians 6:16, I Timothy 3:9, I Timothy 4:6, Hebrews 11:1, Hebrews 11:6, James 17:20, 26, Habakkuk 2:4 and 2 Corinthians 5:7.

As you can see, there are all kinds of issues or reasons one can have from day-to-day for not keeping the faith. But, as you begin to acquire and apply your faith to your daily life, you will see that faith begets faith and through faith we have an unfettered key to God's Throne Room where we are allowed boldly with our requests. We are told that the fervent prayers of a righteous man availeth much. This tells you that prayer is a struggle and you have to wrestle with unseen powers to overcome in order to obtain your requests.

With faith that is ever increasing, one obtains righteousness through Christ Jesus and it is imputed to us as it was Abraham as righteousness. That is how we can come before God as a righteous man or woman and have our prayers overcome the resistance of the enemy. In essence, Christ's faith gives birth to our faith. We are able through this birthing to do all things through Christ with strengthens us.

You and I when endued with Christ by our faith in His Blood, the finished work at the Cross and the empowerment of the Holy Spirit no longer have any spiritual bounds and can achieve total spiritual victory in our daily walk with God by maintaining our submissiveness to Him and His Will for our lives.

NOTES

CHAPTER FOUR

FEAR WILL DESTROY YOUR SPIRITUAL VICTORY

When we look into this study of the word 'fear', most people that are saved tend to instantly think about the fear of the Lord and how we are overcomers of all opposition when we rely upon His power. But the fear that we are speaking of here literally handicaps and cripples young Christians and even mature Christians from fulfilling the purpose of God.

A Christian that does not see God as His Source, power and authority, can be bound by fear in such a way as it literally causes them to freeze right where they are. They will not be able to spiritually move, they cannot spiritually prosper and they are not able to accomplish any small tasks that they may be given charge to carry out. That is why we need to grasp how to overcome fear in our lives.

First of all, one of the ways that you can overcome fear is by having an active prayer life. It is vital that you establish and maintain a sure foundation of Biblical study. It is also imperative that you surround yourself with good brothers and sisters in Christ that can help you to be encouraged and tutor you on how to achieve further victories over various other issues that may arise in your life.

Let's view Psalms 5:7. If you read this verse in its entirety, you will be able to catch the gist of what I am about to say. 'In thy fear will I worship.' We Christians underestimate the power that we can receive from the Holy Spirit by entering into a spirit of worship. When we enter into a spirit of worship, we literally enter into the Throne Room of God and are given vital access to deliver our petitions and requests before the Throne Room of the Lord Jesus.

Psalms 64:1 speaks of the author requesting that God would preserve his life from fear. This really could read 'preserve me from the spirit of fear'. Most often there is a reason for people to be afraid. It can be fear of man, fear of finances, fear of past failings or whatever that fear may be. It most often is accompanied and escorted to a person by a spirit.

2 Timothy 1:7 tells us how we should view fear. It reads, 'For God has not given us the spirit of fear; but of power, and of love, and of a sound mind.' Let's examine this verse in further detail. This speaks of our mental state that we are to mentally dwell not upon fear, but upon the spiritual power that God has endued us with by His infilling of the Holy Spirit. God has filled you not with fear, but with love and a sound mind. A sound mind means 'one that has himself in the sense of spiritual control.' When you think upon these things, remember that perfect love that is imparted to us via the Holy Spirit casteth out all fear. When you view that word 'casteth', it can read 'hurled away.' When something is thrown away, there is distance placed between the one that has thrown the item away and where the item eventually lands and permanently dwells from thereon.

Continuing with the thought of perfect love, we need to look at I John 4:17 and now include verse 18 again. It is very important that as you read your Bible that you build a foundation of Scripture upon Scripture, line upon line and precept upon precept. When you do this, you will find the Bible is an open book and no secret remains. The Scripture is not of private interpretation but has been given to us by the Holy Spirit as a public revelation of the entire person and message of the Lord Jesus Christ.

Continuing with I John 4:17-18, 'Herein is our love made perfect, that we may have boldness in the Day of Judgment: because as He is, so are we in this world. There is no fear in love; but perfect love casts out fear: because fear has torment. He who fears is not made perfect in love.' Read this verse to yourself again silently. Now read it aloud. We are being told a fundamental yet oftentimes oddly overlooked fact. Love is the exact polar opposite of fear. The spirit of love can be made perfect. It gives boldness even during times of battle and during days of judgment. How can you and I have perfect love during our day of judgment when we stand before the Lord? Because our blessed hope is not in what we have done or anything we have tried to accomplish, but we have perfect love and need I say peace because of the finished work that was accomplished once and for all by our Lord and Savior Jesus Christ.

The Lord tells us in these same two verses that we are in this world because He was in this world. And when you think about that, you should start rejoicing because you have victory right at hand. Scripture tells us there is NO fear in love. But let's look at the opposite we were speaking about. Perfect love casteth out fear. Just think about that for a moment. With love, a supernatural love, a manifest love, an imparted love, a love that is given to us only by us being a joint heir with Jesus casts out fear. When you think about casting out, think about the Scriptures in the New Testament when Jesus stood before the possessed. He commanded the foul spirits to come out. But oftentimes the Scripture tells us that He was moved by a spirit of compassion. The same spirit of compassion that set people free from demonic possession can set us free from spiritual oppression that many call the spirit of fear.

Why is it so important that fear be cast out of us? It is not just that we may have a perfect love that we receive from the Lord but because the Lord tells us that in fear there is torment. If you have ever been afraid, there is nothing worse than feeling helpless. We as children of God are not helpless because we are not bound by that spirit. If you are still struggling with the spirit of fear, then you need to realize that you have not yet received your full portion of love because you have not yet allowed God to give you that perfect love.

Romans 8:37 tells us, 'Nay, in all these things we are more than conquerors through Him who loved us. For I am persuaded, that neither death, nor life, nor Angels, nor principalities, nor powers, nor things present, nor things to come, Nor height, nor depth, nor any other creature, shall be able to separate us from the Love of God, which is in Christ Jesus our Lord.' In conclusion, when you read these verses, nothing is mightier than the Cross.

For the Cross bridges the divide that was used to separate God and man. We are now joint heirs with Jesus and have become adopted children of God that when we pray, we can cry out 'Abba Father.' Any good father will not deny their child any good gift. And when we are in need of strength, encouragement and final victory, all we need to do is cry out to our Father which is in Heaven.

When you have access to the Throne of the King and that King is your Father, what can a fallen prince do? The answer is simple. Nothing. You may face battles, you may face trials and you may suffer from fear, but as you continue to seek God and ask Him daily to manifest Himself to you, ask Him to allow His Word to become a living Word in your daily life. You are one step away from becoming a miracle worker in the Kingdom of God.

Notes

 CHAPTER 5

OVERCOMING PAST GUILT

This is probably one of the hardest areas for a Christian to achieve and maintain daily victory. When one thinks of guilt, we often look at everything we have done wrong in the entirety of our lives. From our first wrong choice that we made as a little child to our first open act of willing rebellion against God. Think and look back over your life for just a moment and see where or what is a guilt issue that you as a person and then as a blood-bought, Holy Ghost filled believer have had to deal with. How much guilt do you have stored up in your life?

It depends upon how old you are and how many bad choices you have openly made. People that live a more vocal life or an open one often have more issues to resolve concerning guilt than someone who has lived a more quiet life or a less public one. Public figures or people with high positions of authority have to deal with more external issues of guilt and people that lead more of a quiet life deal with more internal issues of guilt dealing with family, friends and personal relationships. No matter what kind of life you lead, guilt can be that one area in your life that can direct you to make illogical choices. And these choices will ultimately destroy you and your walk with the Lord.

When a person doesn't deal with guilt, it becomes like a cancer that grows. It starts out in the person's mind and then it envelops their daily thoughts and often becomes active in their daily choices. When a Christian fails to deal with guilt or refuses to confront it, then it begins to rot the internal foundation of their relationship with their Lord and Savior.

Guilt to a Christian can be gospel without Christ. Guilt will seek out a place in a believer's mind, heart and spirit. It will seek to blame others for what has been done

(Gen. 3:12-15) and will seek to excuse one's self from his or her own personal choices or responsibilities for what they have done.

When you are finished reading this chapter and you examine your own life, you need to be honest concerning the guilt you allow yourself to carry around. Your guilt will make or break your personal walk with God. It is like carrying a suitcase. At first, it isn't so bad. It's not all that heavy, but then the farther you carry it, the more it weighs and it gets harder and harder to move ahead. Once we allow ourselves to carry guilt around for one thing, then we start to pick up more personal and past guilt and it weighs us completely down. Guilt is a vice that you cannot afford to be indulged in if you desire peace and victory in the Lord.

You may ask, 'How can I deal with my issue of guilt?' Let's look at the word 'issue' for a moment. When the woman with the issue of blood pressed in and said to herself 'if I can just touch the hem of His garment, I can be made whole'. The issue that this woman had started out as a perfectly natural thing. About every thirty days or so, a woman cycles for reproductive reasons. The issue of blood became a problem because it had never left.

It continued to stay with her and began to cause her to lose strength and become more ill by the day. If left untreated, it could have eventually killed this woman. That is exactly what guilt does. It will continue to stay with you and allow yourself to become weak instead of strong in the Lord and weigh you completely down and eventually kill you physically, spiritually and mentally.

God gave us guilt as a part of nature to help keep us in check. Its purpose was to push us to do right and repent of any wrongs. But that is where the problem comes in. Some people just hold on to the guilt instead of dealing with the issues before them. Sooner or later, it leads to spiritual death or mental illness.

So, how can we deal with guilt in a Christian way that will keep us in spiritual victory? First of all, you need to realize that while you view the issue over that of a lifetime, God views it on a day-by-day basis. I John 1:9 is our basis for this. 'If we confess our sins, He is faithful and just to forgive us our sins, and to cleanse us from all unrighteousness.' (KJV) If you confess your sins before Him, then He forgives you right then and there. He cleans you up and makes you new in His sight.

If you have wronged a person, yourself or God, then do not hesitate. Go to God and pray and talk to Him about it. Leave the issue there at the altar with Him and move on. It's His from that point forward. Now, if you have done some wrong to another person, go confess it and be willing to make amends for it. If that person refuses your attempt, then you have done all that you can and you are free and clear before God as long as you have prayed about it and did your best to make things right.

You must learn to forgive yourself again if you have brought an issue to God and resolved it by dealing with the someone you have wronged. At this point, you are no longer guilty of anything because you have done all that a human being can do. Now it is time to move on in the victory of the Lord and stop allowing Satan to beat you over something that you no longer have a need to worry over. John 8:32 says, 'And ye shall know the truth and the truth shall make you free.' (KJV) If you allow yourself to live in the truth, then guilt has no soil whatsoever to grow in your life.

Notes

 CHAPTER 6

DEALING WITH
UNFORGIVENESS IN YOUR LIFE

In this chapter, we will see how we can deal with our past, present and all future issues of unforgiveness. The subject of personal unforgiveness is probably one of the biggest hindrances to a Christian's ability to patch into God's reservoir of blessings that God has laid up for every born-again believer. Until we can come to grips with how to deal with the subject of unforgiveness, then we as believers will be spiritually hindered.

When I speak of unforgiveness, the reader of this chapter needs to comprehend that all of us have dealt with this issue throughout our entire lives. The reason unforgiveness is such a disastrous issue for the Christian is very simple. It literally means that you have refused to move the past into the past. You or I refuse to move forward with God and to seek His present-day personal will for our lives.

We tend to glance backward momentarily which can be devastating because the believers walk with God is to look straight ahead and to always move forward without ever looking behind us.

When you get your eyes off of God even for just a moment, you then lose momentum and may lose sight of the flock. And when we lose sight of the flock, then we oftentimes are on the beginnings of our road to wandering and this leads to more often than not to a cooling down in the soul until one backslides away from the Lord. Part of the problem today for most Christians is that they never grow up and this is because most people today go to a pseudo church that is based upon religion and not upon a daily maturing relationship with God.

Churches today are more worried about numbers of attendees and the size of their buildings and preaching a popular gospel to keep the politics in check than being led by the Holy Spirit of God. Many pastors have latched on to the world's eye view on how the church should act instead of falling on their knees to the Lord in prayer and being led by the Holy Spirit in regards to their mission and vision for the church. And this in part has caused the church to lose touch with some of its basic fundamental teachings one of which is how to deal with unforgiveness.

Let's view a few Scriptures that I use to help myself and others deal with unforgiveness. And be sure if you use these that you pray that the Lord allows you to see the people that you have to deal with concerning unforgiveness as He does. One of my personal favorites is John 3:16. Now, in this very familiar verse, I am always led by the Lord to remember that God died for everyone; especially me. He died for me even when I didn't even know I needed forgiven. He paid the ultimate price for me so that I could escape Hell and eternal separation from Him. So, if God can forgive me who was a sinner saved by grace, how then can I do any less than my Lord Jesus Christ did for me?

Now, here's a few more verses that I use when Satan often tries to infect a soul with hurts and sorrows from the past. (II Chronicles 7:14, Matthew 6:12-15, Matthew 9:6 and Luke 5:21.

You may be saying to yourself, 'Oh, I've been so hurt that I can't forgive.' That is a lie from Satan and it will take you to Hell if you refuse to deal with it! Remember, if God can forgive the ones that crucified Him then who are you to say that you cannot forgive anyone that has mistreated you? Think about that.

Always remember that God is in control and those that hurt His sheep also attack the Shepherd and God is the final authority and will have the final say. Leave it all in His hands and let God be God.

NOTES

 CHAPTER 7

Seeking God's Guidance for Our Lives

In this chapter, we deal with the subject of the born-again believer being led or guided by the Holy Spirit. So many times when I am out preaching, counseling or even witnessing to others about God, I continually hear a familiar refrain, "Where is God in my life? Why does He allow these things to happen to me?" I usually learn very quickly that most of these people that continue to question where God is simply left God out of their discussions or decision-making to begin with and don't even consider including God in their daily lives until everything 'hits the fan.'

There are two kinds of people living in the church for the most part. There are those that have their hand in the Lord's hand on an ongoing daily basis and then there are those that push God out of their daily lives until they need Him and then they are constantly waving their hands to God to rush back into their lives momentarily to rescue and save them. The last group of people is always blaming God for letting them fall into a ditch or blaming Him for everything being in a constant state of confusion in their lives. This is due to the fact that they never study their Bible or refuse to accept it at face value.

They are always trying to interpret into the Bible stuff that is not there or they simply try and remove items that they refuse to accept due to the fact it would interfere with their daily lives. They have no desire to yield an area of their lives to God. This is also known as private rebellion or a secret but loved personal sin.

Let's take a moment to deal with these people that are always confused and blame God for it. Read I Corinthians 14:33, 'For God is not the author of confusion, but of peace, as in all churches of the saints.'(KJV) After reading that verse, you can find a few highlighted areas such as the word 'author'. When you see this word, you can think of a writer that wants his words to be clearly understood by his readers so they might be able to comprehend what is read and transcribe it or repeat it clearly to others around them.

Now the word 'peace' infers to a place of tranquility where the message of the author can take root and prosper. Even in the carnal world one can see that where peace reigns so does prosperity and knowledge. So, let's read this verse again but in a different version. "For God is not the writer of conflict, but of tranquility that the Bride of Christ may dwell in serenity."(DLV)

Most of a person's problems are based upon their own internal failures and their external stimulus. It starts in our own hearts and minds, not by what we see or hear. Now, here's a couple of Scriptures that deals with how God will deal with us as we seek His personal guidance in our daily lives. Psalms 25:14, "The secret of the Lord with them that fear Him; and He will show them His covenant."(KJV) Psalms 27:11, "Teach me thy ways, O Lord, and lead me in a plain path, because of mine enemies."(KJV)

Now, as you view just these two verses, you can see several reasons for any so-called born-again believers to seek the Lord's guidance in his/her daily life. The Lord's way is secret and only shown to those that fear or honor Him and through the Lord Jesus Christ has His covenant been revealed. You must be willing to learn and listen to what the Lord has to say that you may avoid the traps the enemy has laid in front of your path in any given day.

Psalms 32:8 says, "I will instruct thee and teach thee in the way which thou shalt go: I will guide thee with mine eye."(KJV) Psalms 37:5 says, "Commit thy way unto the Lord; trust also in Him; and He shall bring it to pass."(KJV) Psalms 37:33 says, "The steps of a good man are ordered by the Lord."(KJV) And Psalms 78:53 says, "He led them on safely, so they feared not." (KJV)

Let's take a moment to view these verses again and see if we are yet understanding why we need the guidance of the Holy Spirit in our lives. The Lord simply tells us that He would instruct and discipline us in the way and He would guide us where His Spirit leads us. All we have to do is simply look to Him and He will direct our paths. We need to relinquish our lives to Him and rely solely upon Him and He will bring His promises to fruition. He does not fail and His words do not fall void. If you allow God to direct you, then you will be destined by the Spirit of the Lord. The above verses state this very clearly.

Proverbs 3:5-6 tells us to "Trust in the Lord with all of our heart and lean not unto our own understanding. In all thy ways acknowledge Him and He shall direct thy paths."(KJV) No matter what comes our way or what trials we face we just need to trust God and keep our focus on Him. Too many times we think we can handle everything ourselves and pick back up what we left on the altar to God last Sunday at church or in our prayer closet. We think we have the answers and can solve our own problems but we cannot. Our own understanding keeps us in our trials but trusting in God leads us out into victory.

Isaiah 42:16 says, "I will lead them in paths that they have not known: I will make darkness light before them and crooked things straight."(KJV) Isn't it good to know that when we put our all into God that He takes us places that we have never thought we would go and do things we didn't think were possible in our lifetime? All we have to do is place our whole faith in the finished work of Calvary and do not worry or try to reason our lives out. We need to rely upon God entirely and He will direct and keep us. God will take us higher and deeper than our minds can comprehend and the mysteries of God will be illuminated before us and the burdened things will become light.

The Holy Spirit will direct us into God's revealed truths for He does not speak or boast about Himself but of what He has heard that He will speak of and He will reveal the things that must come to pass shortly. God makes provision for those that are called by His name. You can clearly see that you and I must always allow God's Spirit to be a guiding force in our daily lives to avoid the various pitfalls we face in our walk while we yet confront the obstacles that attempt to exalt themselves in our Christian lives as we seek His divine will for our lives.

NOTES

CHAPTER 8

HAVING VICTORY

Having victory is such an easy thing to say for most modern day Christians and yet another thing completely to put into practice. Part of the reason is that so many Christians lose out with God and they fail to keep the victory enabler active in their lives. They don't allow the Holy Spirit to continually renew their daily walk with God. They forget the simple things they can follow from the Bible and more often do not act upon these daily practices.

If you as a born-again believer are having issues in maintaining victory over the world, your flesh or with Satan, then you need to look at the finished work of our Lord and Savior Jesus Christ and His victory which was imparted to us via His grace through the finished work upon the Cross. When you view things through the prism of the Cross, then the Holy Spirit is imparted to you to aid you in your search for victory. Romans 6:14 says, "For sin shall not have dominion over you: for you are not under the law, but under grace."(KJV) We are not subject as believers to the jurisdiction of Satan who for now is the prince of this world. You may be bound by a lot of the issues of Adam and Eve but thanks be to God for the victory He has provided us via His sacrifice upon the Cross. We are and can be delivered and given the victory over any issue we may face. But all of this is dependent upon where you place the cross in relationship to you and God.

The Cross must be the center focal point in your daily walk with the Lord. Everything you do in your life must be in view of the Cross. If you do good works, is it for your glory or His? All that we do, say or think to do must be covered and washed in the blood of the Lamb and then empowered by the blessed Holy Spirit. Any part of this battle for you to maintain victory may be caused by one not keeping their salvation experience current. As long as you keep yourself under the Cross, you will remain saved. This being said, if one sins and fails to repent, he or she will lose their salvation relationship with God and become backslidden and no longer in communion with God. From that point, the person in question would be damned to eternal separation from God should one die in such a state. That means one would be cast into Hell and later the Lake of Fire.

That is your choice. All you have to do is repent once and keep your salvation experience with God current and the way one does this is by spending time with God daily in prayer. One time when I was younger, I was asking for an answer from the Lord for an issue I was facing and I allowed myself to rush my prayers that night and said, 'well, God, if you want to let me know, then I'll be in my bed.' That night true to form, God came to me in a dream and said, "Daren, if you want to hear an answer to a question, then you must talk to someone to hear the answer to that question." And then I woke up and realized that I was so busy asking about the issue, I never truly gave God time to speak to me about the issue. Sometimes we get so wrapped up in a routine that God has to slap us with a loving rebuke to get our attention.

Another way to keep the victory is to testify about what God has done for you to others. This builds your faith and gives God glory and may lead someone else to increase their faith in God. You need to get out of your comfort zone and start witnessing to those around you. Start with your family. This will quickly encourage you to practice what you preach because if you don't, they will surely let you know it and this will be used by the Lord to show you some personal weaknesses you may have. There may be things that you may need to pray through and get the victory over. Then afterwards, you need to move on to your closest friends and then consider some mission trips with your local church. This tends to move one further down the line and allows you to develop gifts and talents you can use for God's glory. As you mature, you will be so busy growing up in God that you don't have time to allow the things of this world to get you down.

Here are some suggestions that you might use to minister:

1. Give out tracts.
2. Teach a class in your church.
3. Go door-to-door with a team to witness.
4. Testify to others as you can.
5. Start a disciple night in your church.
6. Do a nursing home ministry.
7. Be a part of a prison ministry.
8. Go on a mission trip.
9. Get into a daily regiment of Bible study.

When you do a personal bible study, don't just read the verses but take each verse apart word by word and phrase by phrase. Learn to ask your spiritual leaders questions.

Ask more than one person these questions so that they can show you different views and then have them show you how Scripture supports that view. Do not allow opinions to be the object of your study. Exercise the expansion of your mind and the development of your own personal understanding of God's Word and how He would have you apply it into your life.

Psalms 98:1 tells us of how God's power can and will influence our lives via the praise we send up to God. Through our praise, we often empower God to break the hindrances in our lives and thus we will receive the victory from that release. I Corinthians 15:54 shows us that death will one day be finally defeated for those of us that have accepted Jesus Christ as our personal Lord and Savior and that is entirely due to his victory which He has already retained at the Cross of Calvary.

I Corinthians 15:57 literally tells us to be thankful for our Father has provided for us the means to life in abundance by the finished work that was performed by the act of our Lord Jesus Christ. What act?

1. His eternal one-time sacrifice for our sins which were laid upon his back at Calvary.
2. The gifts He provides His church by the Holy Spirit.

3. By His stripes we are healed.
4. You are never alone even in the darkness. He provides light to those that believe.

Maybe you can add a few more that God has placed in your heart what He has done for you or a loved one, a close friend or an acquaintance. I John 5:4 says, "For whatsoever is born of God overcometh the world: and this is the victory that overcometh the world, even our faith."(KJV)

Again, how simple and yet so lost by most in the modern-day church. Why is it lost? Because most in the modern-day church have lost out on that personal experience with God. Faith is the key to this salvation victory experience. In what? The finished work of Jesus Christ upon the Cross. The church must remember that Christ is our Source but He used the Cross as His means to provide grace to us fallen mankind. Faith in Him provides for that grace to be put into activation in our lives and without faith, there is no source or solution to our sin problem.

Too many today have lost their relationship with God because they have allowed a sin situation to develop in their lives. Inch by inch, they have lost their victory in God and sadly, many do not know it until it is already happened. If one ever gets to the point where they think they are perfect, then they need to run to the altar and check themselves to see if they still have all the line of Heaven up and running with God.

Victory is achievable on a daily basis, but we have to entirely depend upon our Lord Jesus Christ and His prescribed method as laid out to us in the Bible.

NOTES

 CHAPTER 9

Maintaining the Fullness of the Holy Ghost in Your Life

When I discuss a believer maintaining the fullness of the Holy Ghost in their life, I am not speaking of just a salvation experience, but one that has been filled to overflowing with the evidence of speaking in other tongues. A believer that is blood-bought has a portion of the Holy Ghost, but not the fullness. And if you don't have the fullness of the Spirit, then you are doing yourself and the rest of the body of your local church a spiritual disservice.

A Spirit-filled believer is a powerful mover and shaker in the spiritual realm. He or she has access to every gift that God has laid up for the church and he or she can have full assurance that these gifts will meet the issues arisen and will be dealt with by the power of the Holy Ghost. A Spirit-filled believer can only maintain his or her fullness of the Holy Ghost by keeping their salvation current. Don't allow your relationship with God to get stale. If you are one of the ones that say that you don't 'feel like you used to when you first got saved' then that tells you that you have got to stop living by the flesh and by feelings and step out and live by faith. In order to avoid a lot of these fleshly issues, one must maintain a regular Bible study. What you feed your spirit-man in the refreshing times is what your spirit-man will be able to draw from in the times of drought.

Bible study and knowledge is the key to keeping oneself encouraged in times of trouble or need. You must keep and maintain a working prayer life. It is one of the primary means by which we maintain our ongoing relationship with God. By prayer, we seek, ask and believe to receive from our Lord and Savior. Prayer opens the windows of Heaven and slams the gates of Hell when we speak to God and He answers us by means of prayer. By prayer, God gives His anointing and lifts burdens and it is via prayer that the Holy Spirit moves and breathes in our lives. Through prayer, the Holy Ghost makes known our needs through groanings that cannot be uttered and healings are bestowed upon those in need. So, when you say, 'I don't have time to pray', then consider this point. The next time your answer seems delayed, it may be due to a lack of Holy Ghost driven prayer power in your life.

In Matthew chapter 3:11, John the Baptist tells us that Jesus would baptize us with the Holy Ghost and fire. Part of the reason we need the fullness of the Holy Ghost is so that He can burn out the dross in our lives and we can maintain a pure and holy life separated from sin and the world. This is sorely needed today and in order to see an end day revival, the true Church is going to have to rise up and say the sin stops here!

Mark chapter 13:11 tells us that in a time of need, the Holy Ghost will lead us as how we should speak and He will give you the words to answer the doubts or questions of unbelievers. Maintaining the Holy Ghost in your life is the key to having Him reveal to you the secrets of the Spirit. Luke 2:26 tells us that Simeon had a revelation that before he would die that the Lord or the Christ would be seen by his eyes.

Luke chapter 12:12 tells us one that is ordered by the Spirit is taught or instructed what they should say in the same hour as the need arises. In the book of John, Jesus 'breathed' upon His disciples and said, 'receive the Holy Ghost.' This for one is a command from Christ to the entirety of the whole body of believers. And if you refuse to seek after the in-filling of the Holy Ghost, then you in effect are living contrary to the will of God in your life.

Notice that the impartation of the Holy Ghost is actually the breath of God filling with his Spirit, power and authority. God breathed into Adam's nose in order that he might become a living soul. So Jesus breathes upon us that we might become a renewed spirit that we might have not only life but life in both the flesh and the Spirit in unfettered abundance.

Acts chapter 1:4 tells us that the Holy Ghost was a promise of the Father spoken of by Jesus. Acts chapter 1:8 tells us why Jesus promised to us the Holy Ghost so His children might have miracle-working power to demonstrate before the world that He is risen. Also that we would be powerful witnesses to a lost and dying world. To let everyone know that He is alive and well and answers prayer.

Romans chapter 14:17 tells us that the Holy Ghost brings about the fullness of the fruits of the Spirit, but it is done by the fullness of joy. The Holy Ghost can bring light into the darkness, a cloud in the time of intense heat, freedom in times of intense oppression and joy that will spring up in the time of overwhelming sorrow.

The Holy Ghost unbeknownst to most of the modern-day church is the very breath of God that we are authorized to speak of. He is the giver by which all power, authority and anointing flows. Without Him, our churches would be just dead and dry pools of sins who would still struggle evermore with the sins of the flesh. The Holy Ghost gives us the power of deliverance and victory over death, Hell and the grave.

Jude 20 tells us to pray in the Spirit because this builds up the believer in the faith. Prayer from our Spirit moves the Spirit of God because when we pray in the Spirit, we are yielded in the Spirit and are allowing God free and full reign over every aspect of our lives which includes our most unruly member-our tongue.

You need to begin to study the Bible for yourself and start maintaining an unhindered Spirit-filled relationship with God. Remember that regardless of what your pastor teaches, the denomination teaches or your own personal choices, the Father has given us a precious gift and that promise is the power to overcome the world. If you refuse such a gift, how can we answer to Christ? The promise of the Father is freely given but you must be willing to yield and accept the gifts of the Spirit as a gift and not an obligation.

The gifts of the Spirit as well as the fruits of the Spirit have been given to us for our benefit and not God's. So I encourage you to strive to maintain a spirit-filled life and ministry that you might impart the gifts of God as a fruitful witness to a lost and dying world.

Notes

 CHAPTER 10

FINDING A SPIRIT-FILLED HOME CHURCH

This chapter is probably one of the most important chapters of the whole book. Finding and having a good Bible-believing, Spirit-filled church is a must in today's world. This world is full of various sins and vices. The modern-day believer needs to find a church where they can be continually refreshed and spiritually fed. Those that are nourished in return can help feed and support fellow believers in the Lord Jesus Christ.

This issue is so vitally important that I could not fail to include it in this book.

When I look out over my past from my childhood days to present, one can truly see that it is a must to be a part of a body of true believers. Spiritual victory in our lives is supported by the help and prayers of our fellow believers. I have noticed in the latter part of the last decade that it has become increasingly hard for true Bible believers in certain parts of the United States to find a well-balanced church. And by that I mean one that will preach forgiveness, love, the gifts of the Spirit, Hell, the soon returning of the Lord, etc. One that will preach the whole gospel, Christ and entirety of the Bible and not just man's assured doctrine. One that will preach the truth that not all churches, faiths and gods or even prophets are created equal. Because, quite frankly, they are not. Scripture clearly tells us there is but one way to Heaven and but one way to the Father and that is through Jesus Christ our Lord. No other name is given by which man may be saved.

It is so apparent that Satan has been on a search and destroy mission trying to beat true Holy Ghost filled churches out of existence. The United States of America may have thousands of church buildings but they have so very few true Bible-believing Christians. And this is due in part to the heads of denominations looking for numbers of churches and attendees instead of numbers of true conversions. They worry about how the world will view their little kingdoms instead of how the Lord will judge them. They forget we are to come out of the world and be separate and then to go and sin no more that we might be blameless in the sight of Christ Jesus instead of being on the right side of what is popular.

It is so bad that currently I myself a minister of the gospel cannot say I honestly have a home church. Since I left my pastoral position at a local church fourteen years ago, I can truly say that all we've been able to do is visit about five or six churches that are ran by brothers in Christ but other than that we've just preached and evangelized as God has given us the opportunity. But we are still actively looking for a good home church to be a place to grow in the Lord and to be a blessing to those around us as well. If you are like me and have had a terrible time finding a good Bible-believing church in your area, then may I suggest that you do the following until you can find a good home church. Don't stop looking for one. Be active and talk to friends and family and see if the know of a good church that you might give a chance to. And remember, give the church a few chances to see how the Spirit moves. See if you and a few others can start a Bible study at your homes. You can start up your own missionary church as long as you have a man or woman that is willing to be led of the Lord and used to deliver a message to the gathered body of believers. You can check out the Internet and see all of the churches in your area as well as any live-streaming services which may be online for you to view any day of the week. Check out the local radio stations for the various preachers in your area. You might want to check out TV for some of the various ministers that will preach to your spiritual needs. All of these venues are a stop gap measure at most except for the Bible study or mission church option. Don't stop looking for a home church.

You will want someone that you can talk and fellowship with and you just can't get that by any other means but by being around other born-again believers that attend a like-minded worship service.

So, keep praying and seeking the will of God for your life and He will direct you in the way to go and when you are around the Spirit of God, you will find the liberty that you have been seeking.

Notes

 ## CHAPTER 11

BRINGING IT
HOME-CLOSING THOUGHTS

In this chapter, I would encourage the reader to go through the book again, but this time with a notebook or a study group and to openly discuss what has been written. Make notes and see if you can add anything of relevance to the chapters. Look up the Scriptures and allow them to bring wisdom to your soul and let them extend the foundation of God in your heart. Remember, this book is only useful if it is truly applied to one's life.

This book that I have written is not about me or my ministry but its about changing the eternal direction of men, women and children to the Lord. It has been my prayer for you who have read this book that God has allowed me to take you further, deeper and yet higher in God and your understanding in His Word and His desire for you to be blessed and prosper in your daily walk with

Him. My book would be a total waste of time if it was all about man's traditions, doctrines or my own thoughts but rather I have sought to give you a book with Scriptures that back up the teachings that will make the reader an evermore victorious believer in Christ Jesus. I have sought to reinforce your beliefs based upon the Word of God and not some mere psycho babble.

When we discussed fear, past guilt or unforgiveness, with the help of the Holy Spirit, I have sought to allow Him to direct me to use Scriptures that will challenge the reader to think, apply and then overcome the challenges they face in their walk with Christ. I have asked God for His holy unction and anointing that I might be able to inspire a small spark in my readers lives that they might catch the flame or vision of God for their lives and pass on the vision of God for this soon to be last end-time great revival.

If you have ignored everything that I have said or taught in this book, please do not ignore this. God is coming back for a people. A true spotless, sinless people. A Bride that is clothed in white that He can take to Himself. You must seek out today a church that preaches the gospel under the direction and power of the Holy Ghost. God is willing to pour out His Spirit still today but is seeking out a people that is fed up with the status quo and desires to seek His face without conditions, terms or deals. A people that will love Him and His Word just because He is. A people that is ready for the last great outpouring, that is ready for God to move the heavens and the Earth one more time.

So, my question to you is this. Are you truly willing to allow God to use you for His purpose and His plan for your life? If so, then victory is just a prayer away. But if you fail to yield, then you may fail to achieve the true victory that you seek. I pray that God truly blesses all of you who read or used this book to teach from and my hope is that you might pass this book on to others so that they may be blessed by it as well.

God bless you all and please uphold myself, my loving wife Kathy and my three sons Adam, Jordan and Justin in your prayers.

Yours until He comes,

Rev. Daren S. Lester